PABLO PICASSO

HUNK OF SKIN

English Versions
by
PAUL BLACKBURN

CITY LIGHTS BOOKS

Library of Congress Catalog Card Number : 68-8390

First American Edition : December, 1968

© 1961 by ' Papeles de Son Armadans '
por amable cesión de Picasso

English translation © 1968 by Paul Blackburn

CITY LIGHTS BOOKS are edited by Lawrence
Ferlinghetti and published at the City Lights Bookstore,
261 Columbus Avenue, San Francisco, California, USA.

NOTE TO THE PRESENT EDITION

Hunk of Skin (Trozo de Piel) is the first Picasso poem written in Spanish to be published. It was written at *La Californie,* the painter's villa in Cannes, January 9, 1959, almost ten years ago now (the first page, the one that begins: 'On the new lush/ grass at the/ well-rim', is dated the day prior). Picasso read me the poem, also at Cannes, June 13, 1960; with him were Jacqueline, his wife, and an American friend, the photographer David Douglas Duncan; with me were two other friends, also Americans: the poet Anthony Kerrigan, who has a very pretty wife and who published *Chronicle of a Voyage to Picasso* in *Papeles de Son Armadans,* No 52, and another contributor, Bob Schiller, who sported a sparse little beard and let a number of atrocious and inconsiderate farts. Bob now has a bar in the Bronx if they haven't killed him yet. I speak of them both, barely disguised, in my *Sheaf of Fables Without Love,* which Picasso illustrated for me. We dined that night at *Chez Felix.*

The title is not Picasso's but mine; the poem was untitled and Picasso told me to baptize it. An edition was made of Poems VII, VIII and IX, with a flower of Jacqueline's as illustration, 88 copies in the *Papeles de Son Armadans* collection; the entire poem was published in 1961 by the *Cuadernos de Maria Cristina*, Málaga, in an edition of 200 copies, and illustrated with four drawings of mine, impossible to reproduce here.

Camilo José Cela
(Mallorca, 1968)

THANKS: The warm and slightly damp gratitude of a still-shaken translator — poor fellow — is offered to Julio Cortázar, who spent a wet Paris afternoon correcting and corroborating the following versions.

—PB
Faro de Cullera
(Valencia)
March, 1968

HUNK OF SKIN

8 . 1 . 59

a la orilla de un pozo sobre la fresca yerba
un incauto mancebo dormia casi desnudo y vestido
de pieles de oso ò de borrego junto á los dos ò tres puntos
cardinales hechos rana y perdiz de fuera y dentro
de las migas puestas à remojar al borde del hornillo
con sus muletas y sus telas de seda encima y sus cubiertos.
de metal y huevo duro mas deprisa y corriendo hecho ascuas
y à tiro de pollo y raja de sandía colgando à cada cuervo.
nada mas y esperando el pandero el ala del pinar
y los flecos de la vela haciendo sus cuentas sobre
la ropa tendida del bosque de piedras recojido
entre las matas de la higuera muerta hechando
sus cuentas debajo del ombligo del almirez ronco
de gritos y zurcidos hechado por debajo
de la puerta escrita à brocha gorda sobre el
trozo de almibar de un cielo puesto de
centinela al borde de la cuna
chispeando migajas y pitos sobre la
casa tirada al mar y mosca del paisaje
frito en la sarten helando sus manos
en el caño del grifo.

8 . 1 . 59

On the new lush
grass at the
well-rim   a
careless young man
was sleeping all
most nude   wearing
skins of lamb or bear
next to the two or three
predetermined cardinal points
frog and partridge outside and in
side crumbs set to soak
next the oven
their muletas and silken
fabrics on top and
their table d'hôte dinners.
of metal and hard boiled
egg and faster and running
made hot coals and close
enuf to shoot a chicken and
a seam of split watermelon
hanging from every
crow.
nothing more
waiting for the tambourine and
the wing of a pine grove and

the fringes of candlelight
making their calculations on
the taut fabric
of stone woods   huddled
among the groves of fig
trees casting their
reckonings under
the belly-button of the mortar hoarse
with cries and mending
slid under the door
writ out with fat brush above
the fragment of syrupy sky
posted as
sentinel   edge of the crib
sparkling out

crumbs and wolf-whistles
over the house
pitched into the sea   the house
fly in the land
scape   fried in the pan
freezing his hands
on the water-faucet
                  spigot.

9 . 1 . 59 :   I

las cajas de betun hacen sus cuentas
tendidas patas abiertas oliendo á
malba clavadas à la puerta del
corral pintadas de ocre y listas
para la fiesta hechas trizas y
cubiertas de pustulas
emborrizadas
en la harina de ojos colgando
de las ristras de chorizos extremeños
tocando el violin enmedio de la
plaza de llantos y congojas del
racimo de boquerones hechos polvos
de arroz y fandangos à la hora del
fuego en el pinar envolviendo
el mantel de cangrejos del pedernal
de la sopa puesta à la ventana
chispeando

9 . 1 . 59 : I

The boxes of
shoeblacking
tot up their reckonings
shins open and out
stretched   smelling of mallows
nailed to the gate of the
corral   painted in bands
of ochre for the fiesta   torn
to shreds and covered with combed out
pimples in the flour of eyes
dangling from strings
of Estremadura chorizos
playing violin in the middle of
the plaza of tears and
anxieties over clusters of sar
dines dusted with rice and fandangos
at the hour of fire
in the pine grove tangling
the tablecloth with crabs
of flint   with soup
set in the window
sparkling

9.1.59: II

luego vino el cartero y el recaudador
de palmas y oles y el ciego de
la parroquia y el mirlo las
niñas de Ramon y las de Doña
Paquita la hija mayor la solterona
y el clerigo estrañados frios
pintados de azafran y verde cargados
de fideos y de huvas negros de
algodon y acibar gordos y muy
derechos hechos rabanos y
sarten llena de huevos con patata
con chicharrones cubiertos de pulgas
y cencerros y la cuestion al ombro
pobres y ricos llevados por la tormenta
sobre el trigo ardiendo mojando
su camisa de granizo la ropa sucia

9 . 1 . 59 :   II

then the mailman came and
the collector of handclapping and olés
and the parish blindman
and the blackbird
Ramon's daughters and doña Paquita's also
the oldest daughter   the old maid
and the priest standing coldly apart painted
saffron and green
loaded with noodles and black
grapes of cotton and aloes   fat and
very erect   become radishes and
fryingpan full of eggs
and home fries   fried
cracklings covered with fleas
and cattle bells and the question
carried on the shoulder   poor
and rich swept off by the rainstorm
above the burning wheat   soaking
his shirt with
hail   the dirty linen

9 . 1 . 59 :   III

la mayor la Filis la que yá le cuecen las
pulgas se puso tonta y se hechó en la
cama vestida de lo que era se tragó las
las lagrimas y los suspiros y se hecho encima
el colchon y el perro de porcelana para
hacerse pasar por Mesalina que no es
lo creyó el hijo del alcalde y
el ventero que se pusieron locos de
contento tocando el uno el pandero
y el otro el rabel à salpicones
sobre el vestido y los encajes que
le colgaban entre las piernas de
las persianas entornadas del cuarto
escaleras de Sol para paseo de
moscas y oro en polvareda de agua
de azaar y de la madre Celestina

9 . 1 . 59 :   III

Phyllis
the oldest one
her fleas itching already
got stupid and threw herself
into bed dressed
in what she was wearing   the
tears
and sighs
and threw herself down
on top of the mattress
and the porcelain dog so as to
pass for Messalina   which
she is not   as the mayor's son
and the innkeeper believed   who went
crazy with happiness
one banging the tambourine   the other
the rebec   splashing music
over the suit and the laces
hanging between the legs of
the Venetian
blinds half-open into
the room making
stairways of SUN for
flies taking afternoon walks
and gold in a dustcloud of water

orange blossoms and Celestina's
mother   sheer magic
powders

9 . 1 . 59 : IV

cuando el cartero supo lo que la niña hacia
sobre el paño trigueño del terciopelo
azul del monton de zapos que debajo
del acardenalado turquí resaba el
pedazo de capa manchado de coral
del trapo la bola de jazmín pitando
sus anforas y sus bueyes rehizo sus
acrobaticas zandeces y enrredó
la trama — No faltó mas que
la llegada de la madre coronela y sus
niñas para que la funcion le
estayase en la mano la chica
se enrredó en sus cuentas y
le salió un grano en el trasero
y no por orden y ordenanza de lo
que Dios manda ni reconocimiento farmaceutico
y aun menos para hacer gracia

9 . 1 . 59 :   IV

when the mailman figured
out what the little girl was doing
on the brownish velvet cloth blue
from the flock of toads praying under
neath the black/an/blue turquoise the
piece of cloak stained coral from the rag
the ball of jasmine
to whistle up their
amphoras and their oxen
he did his silly acrobatics again
and ran afoul of the plot —
Nothing missing but the
arrival of the queen mother colonel
and her daughters
so that the function blew up in the hand
the girl got all tangled up in her calculations
and a seed jumped out and up her rump, not
to order or
by ordinance
as God ordains
nor by pharmaceutical recognition
certainly not
just to be pleasant

9 . 1 . 59 : V

ni para hacerse pasar por chistosa ni
viva acaramelada y duende si nó por
haber tenido la hora que pasaba cojida
por el gaznate y tragarle la lengua
al pez y hacer cosquillas
al chico y el abuelo subidos en
burro vistos muy lejos à lo lejos del
camino rascando el polvo à zapatasos
que nadie hubiese dicho ni hecho ni
deshecho ni clavado ni desclavado del
erizo pues al menor ruido y à la
primera gota de lluvia el saco de
harina hubiese mojado su cabellera
en el caldero y hubiese hecho de
montaña un cascabel y crujir el
rosal sobre el mar de la mesa
puesta con la sopa el porron el
pan las cucharas el cuchillo los tomates y su cara.

9.1.59: V

nor ought it be
thought a joke
nor wisecrack
nor sugar-sweet nor
goblin if not for
having seized the passing
hour limping along at the top of its lungs
swallowing the fish's tongue
and tickling the boy and his grandfather
climbing onto the burro
seen very far off to the far
reaches of the road
scratching in the dust
stomping
for no one would have
said or done
or undone
nailed down or
pulled out
the porcupine's quills since
at the slightest noise
at the first drop of rain
the flour sack would have soaked her
tresses in the kettle
would have

made the mountain
a tinkle bell
and to crunch the rosebush
upon the sea of
the table set
with the soup
the *porron*
the bread the
spoons
the knife the
tomatoes and
her face

9 . 1 . 59 : VI

no hay bien que por mal no venga dijo
el remendon ni verguenza que se
desuelle à la ventana las rajas y tajadas
de sol lamen los barrotes de las sillas
lloronas à lo largo de la tarde clavileña
en un rincon justiciero de la luz
arrastrada por las mulillas.
à carcajada limpia la murga del alba cauterisa
la llaga hecha por los dedos en la piel
de la tarde en el cielo color de mostaza
pintado de cobalto pisando el pan
verde de la arena amapola retorciendo
sus bailes.
A las 4 de la tarde no à las 5 el
relampago de la llegada de la hija del tio
vivo arregló la tinta en la sopera la luz
se puso tibia y de sopeton se hechó à
perder el baile con el tio

9.1.59: VI

Every silver
lining has its
dark cloud said
the cobbler   and
you don't skin your
mother in the open
window
the splinters and splices of sun
licking the chair rungs   crying
the whole rockinghorse afternoon in
an austere corner the
light
harrowed by mules.
with a clean peal of laughter
the dawn's brass
band cauterizes the wound
the fingers made in the skin
of afternoon
in the mustard-colored
sky painted cobalt
trampling underfoot
the green bread
of the poppy sand
twisting its dances

At 4 in the afternoon
not at 5 the
lightning-swift arrival of
the merry-go-round
's daughter
fixes the colors in the tureen
the light grows
indifferent and
suddenly
it went sour the
dance with the merry-go-
uncle

9 . 1 . 59 : VII

Ajonjolin hecho sopa y mas borracho que
una cuba y un jaleo de primera de segunda
y de tercera hechando chispas y capirotes
renegando y tociendo meandose encima
del piano y tirandose pedos en el cornetin
su mujer la jacinta la burra y la santa
lloraba y se arrancaba las barbas del papel
de estraza arrugado que amordazaban
sus patas de cangrejo entre sus faldas
los ostiones pequeños y hijos lejitimos
y de legitìmo matrimonio juanito enrique
y Baldomero pues no faltaria mas
si los pinceles sucios no rascacen la
paleta de odios y esperanzas el archibo
de eructaciones que un padre y una
madre recuecen en el puchero de
alegria y jolgorio de un dia de fiesta
à punto de caramelo.

9.1.59 : VII

Sesame
drenched to the ears and
drunk as a skunk and balling
of the first water
and of the second and
of the third throwing
off sparks and plenty of action
cursing and coughing
peeing on top of the
piano farting   into the cornet
his wife
Ruby
she-ass and saint
was weeping
pulling at the rough edges of
the wrinkled rag paper that was
swathing her crab's legs under
her skirts   tiny oysters
and legitimate sons from legitimate matrimony
Johnny   Henry   and
Baldomero
So that would have been okay
if the dirty brushes were
not scraping hopes and hates
off the palette   the

whole filing cabinet full of
belches that a father and
mother boil over
and over again in
the pot of joy
the ebullience of a fiesta day
on the point of   becoming
caramel candy.

9.1.59 : VIII

Un zapato de queso una bota de arroz
un par de huevos un nido de caracoles
un cepillo y un pollo un canario
y una codorniz un florero un tintero
un real de vellon un mirlo
un cuento un lapiz un botijo un
valon una gallina ciega la
historia de la madre celestina
y una cuadrilla de niños sevillanos
toreros el tio Periquito los otros
y los demas allá el perro de san
Roque tres cuatro la mitad y
el cuarto el mar y las olas y los
peces el campo y los corderos las
vacas y los toros Lagartijo y las
lagartijas los 4 niños de Ecija
almendras castañas nueces avellanas
y pasas perdices codornices jilgueros
albaaca tomillo romero alucema

9 . 1 . 59 :　VIII

One cheese shoe
one boot of rice
pair of eggs a
nest of snails
one brush and
one chicken
a canary
one quail
a flowerpot
an inkpot　　a
plugged nickel
a blackbird
a story
a pencil
a jug　　one
Walloon one
blind hen the
history of mother Celestina
and a cuadrilla of kids from Sevilla
bullfighters
uncle Parrakeet
the others and the rest there
San Roque's dog three four one-half and
one-quarter
the sea and the waves and the fish

the countryside and the lambs
the cows
and the bulls
Lagartijo the matador and the
lady lizards
Ecija's   4   kids, almonds
chestnuts   walnuts   hazelnuts
and raisins
partridges
quail
linnets
basil
thyme   rosemary
lavender

9 . 1 . 59 :   IX

humo de hierba seca tio vivo alambres
piedra madera y cal vino tinto
solera aguardiente y conejo aceitunas
mesa silla botella vaso ladrillo arena
pimienta y sal limon naranja
camisa camiseta calzoncillo medias
y calcetines piedras y piedras y mas
piedras y tal y tal y cual y tal
y cual y tal y tal y qual y qual
y tal y 1 y 2 . y 3 . y 4 y 5 y 6
y 7 y 8 y 9 y 10 y 11 y 12 y 13
y 14 y 15 y 16 y 17 y 18 y 19
y 20 y 21 y 22 y 23 y 24 y 25
y 26 y 27 y 28 y 29 y 30 y 31 y 32 y 33
y 34 y 35 y 36 y 37 y 38 y 39 y 40 y 41
y 42 y 43 y 44 y 45 y . . .

9 . 1 . 59 : IX

smoke of dried herbs
merry-go-round
wires
stone
wood and whitewash
red wine
lees
hard liquor rabbit
olives table
chair bottle glass
brick
sand
black pepper and salt lemon
orange shirt
undershirt
under drawers stockings
and socks stones
and stones and more
stones and such and such and so and such
and so and such and such and so and so
and such and 1 and 2.   and 3.   and 4 and 5 and 6
and 7 and 8 and 9 and 10 and 11 and 12 and 13 and
14 and 15 and 16 and 17 and 18 and 19
and 20 and 21 and 22 and 23 and 24 and 25
and 26 and 27 and 28 and 29 and 30 and 31 and 32

and 33
and 34 and 35 and 36 and 37 and 38 and 39 and 40
and 41
and 42 and 43 and 44 and 45 and . . .

CITY LIGHTS BOOKS

Artaud, Antonin. ANTHOLOGY
Bowles, Paul. A HUNDRED CAMELS IN THE COURTYARD
Burroughs, William & Ginsberg, Allen. THE YAGE LETTERS
CITY LIGHTS JOURNAL (No. 3)
Corso, Gregory. GASOLINE
Cossery, Albert. MEN GOD FORGOT
Dahlberg, Edward. BOTTOM DOGS
Daumal, René. MOUNT ANALOGUE
David-Neel, Alexandra. SECRET ORAL TEACHINGS IN TIBETAN BUDDHIST SECTS
Fenollosa, Ernest. THE CHINESE WRITTEN CHARACTER AS A MEDIUM FOR POETRY
Ferlinghetti. PICTURES OF THE GONE WORLD (PP. No. 1)
Ginsberg, Allen. HOWL AND OTHER POEMS (PP. No. 4)
Ginsberg, Allen. KADDISH AND OTHER POEMS (PP. No. 14)
Ginsberg, Allen. PLANET NEWS (PP. No. 23)
Ginsberg, Allen. REALITY SANDWICHES (PP. No. 18)
Hollo, Anselm. (Tr.) RED CATS (PP. No. 16)
Kaufman, Bob. GOLDEN SARDINE (PP. No. 21)
Kerouac, Jack. BOOK OF DREAMS
Lamantia, Philip. SELECTED POEMS (PP. No. 20)
Lowry, Malcolm. SELECTED POEMS (PP. No. 17)
Mailer, Norman. THE WHITE NEGRO
McClure, Michael. MEAT SCIENCE ESSAYS
Michaux, Henri. MISERABLE MIRACLE
O'Hara, Frank. LUNCH POEMS (PP. No. 19)
Olson, Charles. CALL ME ISHMAEL
Patchen, Kenneth. LOVE POEMS (PP. No. 13)
Patchen, Kenneth. POEMS OF HUMOR & PROTEST (PP. No. 3)
Pommy-Vega, Janine. POEMS TO FERNANDO (PP. No. 22)
Prévert, Jacques. PAROLES (PP. No. 9)
Rexroth, Kenneth. BEYOND THE MOUNTAINS
Rexroth, Kenneth (Tr.). THIRTY SPANISH POEMS OF LOVE & EXILE (PP. No. 2)
Sanders, Ed. POEM FROM JAIL
Shure, Robert. TWINK
Solomon, Carl. MISHAPS, PERHAPS
Solomon, Carl. MORE MISHAPS
Svevo, Italo. JAMES JOYCE
Topor, Roland. PANIC (Drawings)
Watts, Alan W. BEAT ZEN, SQUARE ZEN, AND ZEN
Williams, William Carlos. KORA IN HELL: IMPROVISATIONS (PP. No. 7)